D0349502

WEIRD THINGS CUSTOMERS SAY IN BOOKSHOPS

WEIRD THINGS CUSTOMERS SAY IN BOOKSHOPS

Jen Campbell

CONSTABLE

Constable & Robinson Ltd
55-56 Russell Square
London WC1B 4HP

This edition published by Constable,
an imprint of Constable & Robinson Ltd 2012

Copyright © Jen Campbell 2012

Illustrations copyright © The Brothers McLeod 2012

All rights reserved. This book is sold subject to the condition that it shall not, by way of trade or otherwise, be lent, re-sold, hired out or otherwise circulated in any form of binding or cover other than that in which it is published and without a similar condition including this condition being imposed on the subsequent purchaser.

A copy of the British Library Cataloguing in Publication Data is available from the British Library

ISBN-13: 978-1-78033-483-7

Printed and bound in the European Union

5 7 9 10 8 6 4

For bookshops and heroic booksellers everywhere
with thanks to our loyal customers,
without whom we wouldn't be selling books
&
to all the people within these pages
who've kept me on my toes,
made me smile and scared
the absolute hell out of me – thank *you*.

CONTENTS

TALES FROM

The Edinburgh Bookshop

The Edinburgh Bookshop [formerly The Children's Bookshop], Bruntsfield Place, Edinburgh, is an independent bookshop owned by Vanessa and Malcolm Robertson, also owners of Fidra Books publishing company. Their bookshop dog is Teaga, a Leonberger, who somewhat resembles Nana from Peter Pan.

www.edinburghbookshop.com.

CUSTOMER: I read a book in the sixties. I don't remember the author, or the title. But it was green, and it made me laugh. Do you know which one I mean?

♦

CUSTOMER: Hi, I'd like to return this book, please.
BOOKSELLER: Certainly. Do you have the receipt?
CUSTOMER: Here.
BOOKSELLER: Erm, you bought this book at Waterstone's.
CUSTOMER: Yes.
BOOKSELLER: . . . we're not Waterstone's.
CUSTOMER: But you're a bookshop.
BOOKSELLER: Yes, but we're not Waterstone's.
CUSTOMER: You're all part of the same chain.
BOOKSELLER: No, sorry, we're an independent bookshop.
CUSTOMER: . . .
BOOKSELLER: Put it this way, you wouldn't buy clothes in H&M and take them back to Zara, would you?
CUSTOMER: Well, no, because they're different shops.
BOOKSELLER: Exactly.
CUSTOMER: . . . I'd like to speak to your manager.

CUSTOMER: My children are just climbing your bookshelves. That's ok, isn't it? They won't topple over, will they?

CUSTOMER: It makes me sad that grown up books don't have pictures in them. You're brought up with them when you're younger, and then suddenly they're all taken away.
BOOKSELLER: . . . Yes. It's a cruel world.

♦

CUSTOMER: Do you have any books by Jane Eyre?

♦

CUSTOMER: Hi, I just wanted to ask: did Anne Frank ever write a sequel?
BOOKSELLER: ……..
CUSTOMER: I really enjoyed her first book.
BOOKSELLER: Her diary?
CUSTOMER: Yes, the diary.
BOOKSELLER: Her diary wasn't fictional.
CUSTOMER: Really?
BOOKSELLER: Yes... She really dies at the end – that's why the diary finishes. She was taken to a concentration camp.
CUSTOMER: Oh... that's terrible.
BOOKSELLER: Yes, it was awful -
CUSTOMER: I mean, it's such a shame, you know? She was *such* a good writer.

CUSTOMER: Do you have any crime books involving speeding fines?

♦

CUSTOMER *(to her friend)*: What's this *literary criticism* section? Is it for books that complain about other books?

♦

CUSTOMER: Do you have a copy of *Nineteen Eighty Six*?
BOOKSELLER: *Nineteen Eighty Six*?
CUSTOMER: Yeah, Orwell.
BOOKSELLER: Oh – *Nineteen Eighty Four.*
CUSTOMER: No, I'm sure it's *Nineteen Eighty Six*; I've always remembered it because it's the year I was born.
BOOKSELLER: . . .

WOMAN: Hi, where are your copies of *Breaking Dawn*? I can't see any on the shelf.
BOOKSELLER: Sorry, I think we've sold out of the *Twilight* books; we're waiting on more.
WOMAN: What?
BOOKSELLER: We should have some more in tomorrow.
WOMAN: But I need a copy now. I finished the third one last night.
BOOKSELLER: I'm sorry, I can't help you.
WOMAN: No, you don't understand, I've taken the whole day off work to read it.
BOOKSELLER: Erm . . .
WOMAN: I NEED TO KNOW WHAT HAPPENS! NOW!
BOOKSELLER: Erm . . .
WOMAN: Can you call your wholesaler and see if they can deliver this afternoon?
BOOKSELLER: They only—
WOMAN: And then I can wait here for them.
BOOKSELLER: I'm sorry, they only deliver in the morning.
WOMAN: BUT WHAT AM I SUPPOSED TO DO NOW?
BOOKSELLER: . . . we have many other books.
WOMAN *(sniffs)*: Do any of those have Robert Pattinson in them?

♦

CUSTOMER: Do you have any books in this shade of green, to match the wrapping paper I've bought?

CUSTOMER: These books are really stupid, aren't they?
BOOKSELLER: Which ones?
CUSTOMER: You know, the ones where animals like cats and mice are best friends.
BOOKSELLER: I suppose they're not very realistic, but then that's fiction.
CUSTOMER: They're more than unrealistic; they're really stupid.
BOOKSELLER: Well, writers use that kind of thing to teach kids about accepting people different to themselves, you know?
CUSTOMER: Yeah, well, books shouldn't pretend that different people get on like that and that everything is 'la de da' and wonderful, should they? Kids should learn that life's a bitch, and the sooner the better.

CUSTOMER: Do you have that book – I forget what it's called; it's about people with large, hairy feet.
BOOKSELLER: Do you mean hobbits? *The Lord of the Rings*?
CUSTOMER: No.... erm – The Hairy Bikers.

♦

CUSTOMER: My granddaughter's looking for a book about Agnes's knickers.. do you know what I mean?
BOOKSELLER: Agnes's knickers... Ah! Louise Rennison can be found over here.
[*Angus, Thongs and Full-Frontal Snogging*]

♦

CUSTOMER: Do you have any pop-up books on sex education?

CUSTOMER: You know how they say that if you gave a thousand monkeys typewriters, then they'd eventually churn out really good writing?
BOOKSELLER: . . . yes.
CUSTOMER: Well, do you have any books by those monkeys?
BOOKSELLER: . . .

♦

CUSTOMER *(holding up a copy of a Harry Potter book)*: This doesn't have anything weird in it... does it?
BOOKSELLER: You mean, like, werewolves?
CUSTOMER: No *(whispers)* - gays.
BOOKSELLER: . . . right.

CUSTOMER: I'm just going to nip to the supermarket to do the weekly shop. I'm going to leave my sons here, is that ok? They're three and five. They're no bother.

♦

CUSTOMER: Do you have a book with a list of careers? I want to give my daughter some inspiration.
BOOKSELLER: Ah, is she applying to university?
CUSTOMER: Oh no, not yet. She's just over there. Sweetheart?
(a four year old girl comes over)
CUSTOMER: There you are. Now, you talk to the nice lady, and I'm going to find you a book on how to become a doctor or a scientist. What do you think about that?
(The girl says nothing)
CUSTOMER *(to bookseller)*: Won't be a sec.
(Customer wanders off into non-fiction)
BOOKSELLER: So, what's your name?
CHILD: Sarah.
BOOKSELLER: Sarah? That's a beautiful name.
CHILD: Thank you.
BOOKSELLER: So, Sarah, what do *you* want to be when you grow up?
CHILD: . . . A bumblebee.
BOOKSELLER: Excellent.

CUSTOMER: I do find it odd that people manage to make a living out of writing books for children. I'm sure any mother could do it.
BOOKSELLER: Why don't you try it yourself?
CUSTOMER: I always mean to, but I'm very busy right now with my pottery class.

♦

(Local author comes into bookshop, lifts his books from the bookshelf and starts rearranging them on the table in the middle of the room)
BOOKSELLER: What are you doing?
LOCAL AUTHOR: Well, they're never going to sell when they're sitting on a bookshelf, are they?

♦

CUSTOMER: I'm looking for a book for my son. He's six.
BOOKSELLER: How about this one – it's about—
CUSTOMER: Yeah, whatever, I'll take it.

CUSTOMER: You know that film, *Coraline*?
BOOKSELLER: Yes, indeed.
CUSTOMER: My daughter loves it. Are they going to make it into a book?

CUSTOMER: If my daughter wants to buy books from the teenage section do you need to see some form of ID? It was her thirteenth birthday this weekend. I can show you pictures of the cake. You can count the candles.

CUSTOMER: Are all of your books for sale, or just some of them?

CUSTOMER: Do you have any medical textbooks?
BOOKSELLER: Sorry, no. They go out of date so quickly we don't stock them, but I can order one in for you.
CUSTOMER: I'm not worried about it being in date.
BOOKSELLER: Does your university not request you have a specific edition?
CUSTOMER: Oh, I'm not a medical student, I just want to learn how to do stitches.
BOOKSELLER: ...Right.
CUSTOMER: Do you have a book on sewing, instead?

(Customer comes into the shop with her five year old son)
CUSTOMER: Come on, Alfie, take your shoes off.
BOOKSELLER: It's OK... you don't have to take your shoes off to come into the bookshop.
CUSTOMER: Please don't encourage him. I'm trying to train him to remember to take his shoes off in the house because we've got new carpets. The more he does it, the more he'll remember.

♦

CUSTOMER: Do you have a copy of *Bridget Jones: The Edge of Reason*? I can't see it on the shelf.
BOOKSELLER: I'm afraid we don't, but I can order it for you, and it'll be here in the next forty eight hours. We could even post it to you if you'd like?
CUSTOMER: I don't trust the Royal Mail. Could you fax it instead?

♦

CUSTOMER: Do you have any books signed by Margaret Atwood?
BOOKSELLER: We have many Margaret Atwood books, but I'm afraid we don't have any signed by Margaret Atwood, no.
CUSTOMER: I'm looking for a birthday present for my wife. I know she'd really love a signed copy. You couldn't fake a signature could you?

CUSTOMER: Which was the first *Harry Potter* book?
BOOKSELLER: *The Philosopher's Stone.*
CUSTOMER: And the second?
BOOKSELLER: *The Chamber of Secrets.*
CUSTOMER: I'll take *The Chamber of Secrets.* I don't want *The Philosopher's Stone.*
BOOKSELLER: Have you already read that one?
CUSTOMER: No, but with series of books I always find they take a while to really get going. I don't want to waste my time with the useless introductory stuff at the beginning.
BOOKSELLER: The story in *Harry Potter* actually starts right away. Personally, I do recommend that you start with the first book – and it's very good.
CUSTOMER: Are you working on commission?
BOOKSELLER: No.
CUSTOMER: Right. How many books are there in total?
BOOKSELLER: Seven.
CUSTOMER: Exactly. I'm not going to waste my money on the first book when there are so many others to buy. I'll take the second one.
BOOKSELLER: . . . If you're sure.

(One week later, the customer returns)
BOOKSELLER: Hi, did you want to buy a copy of *The Prisoner of Azkaban?*
CUSTOMER: What's that?
BOOKSELLER: It's the book after *The Chamber of Secrets.*
CUSTOMER: Oh, no, definitely not. I found that book far too

confusing. I ask you, how on earth are children supposed to understand it if I can't? I mean, who the heck is that Voldemort guy anyway? No. I'm not going to bother with the rest.
BOOKSELLER: . . .

♦

CUSTOMER: Where are your fictional novels?

♦

CHILD: Mummy, can we buy this book?
MOTHER: Put that down, Benjamin. We've got quite enough books at home!

Phone rings.
BOOKSELLER: Hello.
CUSTOMER: Hi. I was wondering if you could help me. I'm looking for a book for my niece. She's six and I've no idea what to buy her.
BOOKSELLER: Sure. What kinds of things is she in to?
CUSTOMER: I don't really know. I don't see her very often – my sister lives abroad.
BOOKSELLER: OK, what's her name?
CUSTOMER: Sophie.
BOOKSELLER: Ah, well, have you considered the Dick King Smith *Sophie* series? There's even a book called *Sophie's Six.*
CUSTOMER: OK, sure, that sounds like a good idea.
BOOKSELLER: Do you want me to double check that we have those in stock? I'm pretty sure we do.
CUSTOMER: No, it's OK. I'm just going to order them online.
BOOKSELLER: But... we just gave you the recommendation.
CUSTOMER: I know, and I appreciate it. It's a pain that Amazon don't have a physical person I can ask about this sort of thing. Still, I can always rely on you guys for advice.
BOOKSELLER: . . .

♦

CUSTOMER: Do you keep the pornography in the photography section? –

CUSTOMER: Did Charles Dickens ever write anything fun?

(A child is playing with a book on the floor and rips it)
CHILD'S MOTHER: Oh, Stephen *(she tuts in a non-serious way)*. Do be careful. *(She takes the book off the child and puts it back on the shelf)*
BOOKSELLER: Excuse me?
CHILD'S MOTHER: Yes?
BOOKSELLER: Your son just ripped the head off the tiger who came to tea.
CHILD'S MOTHER: I know. Children, ey?
BOOKSELLER: Yes, but we can't sell that book now. It's damaged.
CHILD'S MOTHER: Well I don't know what you expect *me* to do about it.

♦

CUSTOMER: I'm looking for a book for my eleven year old daughter. What would you recommend? I'd like something educational, too, not anything nonsensical.
BOOKSELLER: Well, how about something like *When Hitler Stole Pink Rabbit?* She'll be doing the second world war at school soon, and this is about Judith Kerr's life. She had to travel across Europe when she was a little girl because her father was a German journalist outspoken against Hitler, and it's about her settling in to schools in France and England, and learning new languages.
CUSTOMER: I don't really want her to learn about all that Hitler Nazi nonsense. It's all so long ago, now, and completely irrelevant. It's tedious.

CUSTOMER: Is this book edible?
BOOKSELLER: … No.

♦

CUSTOMER: Do you run story time for children?
BOOKSELLER: Yes, we do. It's on a Tuesday, for toddlers.
CUSTOMER: Great, the crèche up the road is so expensive, and I've been dying to have a few hours to go shopping, and maybe get my nails done.
BOOKSELLER: I'm sorry, but I'm afraid you have to supervise your child at story time.
CUSTOMER: Why?
BOOKSELLER: . . . because we're *not* a crèche.

CUSTOMER *(shouting from the doorway)*: Do you have any jobs going at the moment? I'd come in and talk properly, but I'm really busy.

♦

CUSTOMER: Doesn't it bother you, being surrounded by books all day? I think I'd be paranoid they were all going to jump off the shelves and kill me.
BOOKSELLER: . . .

BOOKSELLER: Can I help at all?
CUSTOMER: Yes, where's your fiction section?
BOOKSELLER: It starts over on the far wall. Are you looking for anything in particular?
CUSTOMER: Yes, any books by Stefan Browning.
BOOKSELLER: I'm not familiar with him, what kind of books has he written?
CUSTOMER: I don't know if he's written any. You see, my name's Stefan Browning, and I always like to go into bookshops to see if anyone with my name has written a book.
BOOKSELLER: . . . right.
CUSTOMER: Because then I can buy it, you see, and carry it around with me and tell everyone that I've had a novel published. Then everyone will think I'm really cool, don't you think?
BOOKSELLER: . . .

♦

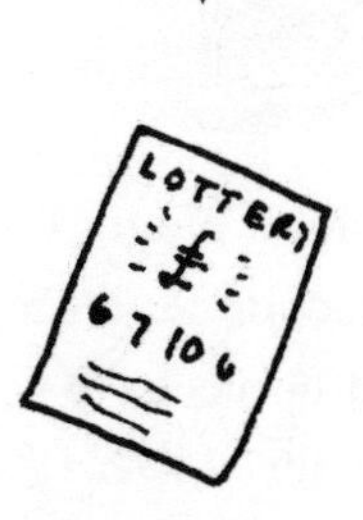

CUSTOMER: This might be a stupid question, but do you sell milk?

CUSTOMER: Do you sell lottery tickets?

CUSTOMER: Do you sell screw drivers?

CUSTOMER: Do you have an LGBT fiction section?
BOOKSELLER: We don't have a specific section, but we do have LGBT literature – Sarah Waters, Ali Smith, Jeanette Winterson, Christopher Isherwood etc. Which author were you looking for?
CUSTOMER: Don't worry, I'll have a look through the fiction section – thanks for your help.
OTHER CUSTOMER: Sorry, did I hear you right? Did you just say that all the homosexual books are in with the normal fiction.
BOOKSELLER: All our fiction is one section.
(Other Customer looks suspiciously at the book she's holding and slides it back on the shelf)

♦

CUSTOMER: I'm looking for a biography to read that's really interesting. Could you recommend one?
BOOKSELLER: Sure. What books have you read and liked?
CUSTOMER: Well, I really loved *Mein Kampf.*
BOOKSELLER: . . .
CUSTOMER: Loved is probably not the right word.
BOOKSELLER: No. Probably not.
CUSTOMER: Liked, is probably better. Yes. Liked. I liked it a lot.
BOOKSELLER: . . .

CUSTOMER: Didn't this place used to be a camera shop?
BOOKSELLER: Yes, it did, but we bought the place a year ago.
CUSTOMER: And now you're a . . .
BOOKSELLER: . . . a bookshop.
CUSTOMER: Right. Yes. So, where do you keep the cameras?

♦

CUSTOMER: Do you have any books on the story of Easter?
BOOKSELLER: I'm sure we do, yes.
CUSTOMER: Excellent. Something with lots of chicks and rabbits would be great, thanks.

CUSTOMER: Do you have a book which lists the weather forecast for the rest of this year?

♦

CUSTOMER: Will you be open so I can buy the new Harry Potter book?
BOOKSELLER: Yep, we're having a midnight opening.
CUSTOMER: Great. What time?

CUSTOMER: Do you have a book of mother-in-law jokes? I want to give it to my mother-in-law as a joke. But, you know, not really as a joke at all.

CHILD: Mum, look, it's the book of *A Hundred and One Dalmatians.* Can I get a hundred and one puppies?
CHILD'S MOTHER: No, dear, you've already got a hamster. That's quite enough.

CUSTOMER: I'm looking for a book for my son. He's only seven but he's so advanced; it's like he has the brain of a twenty year old. What would you recommend?

(Child finds the light switch and begins to flick it on and off... and on and off)
CHILD'S MOTHER: He's playing a game he calls 'Night and Day.'
BOOKSELLER: Could you please ask him to stop? I need to be able to see the till to serve these customers.
CHILD'S MOTHER: It's ok. He'll stop in a few minutes. See, he's pretending to snore at the moment. He'll stop soon and pretend to wake up, and switch the light on like it's the sun. He's so imaginative, isn't he? David, what time is it in the game?
CHILD: It's five in the morning!
CHILD'S MOTHER *(to bookseller)*: See. Not long to go now. Just be patient.

♦

CUSTOMER: Do you have any positions available at the moment? I'd like my daughter to get a Saturday job.
BOOKSELLER: If your daughter is interested in working for us, it'd be best if she came and spoke to us herself.
CUSTOMER: I don't think she's that keen on having a job, that's the problem... But you could always come round to our house and try and convince her to come and work for you. Then she might consider it.

CUSTOMER: Do you have a copy of *Atonement*? But not the film cover, please. Keira Knightley's neck makes me want to punch things.

♦

CUSTOMER: I'd like a refund on this book please.
BOOKSELLER: What seems to be the problem?
CUSTOMER: It's broken! I barely touched it. It's ridiculous!
BOOKSELLER: What do you mean?
CUSTOMER: I *mean* all I did was drop it in the bath by accident. And now, I mean, just *look* at it: the thing's unreadable!

CUSTOMER: Do you have any books containing passages which would be suitable to read out at a funeral?
BOOKSELLER: Sure, I'll help you look.
CUSTOMER: Thanks.
BOOKSELLER: And I'm sorry for your loss.
CUSTOMER: Oh, don't worry about it, it's just my daughter's guinea pig.

CUSTOMER *(holding up a Jamie Oliver cookbook):* Would you mind if I photocopied this recipe?
BOOKSELLER: Yes, I would.

CUSTOMER: Where's your poetry section?
BOOKSELLER: It's just over here.
CUSTOMER: Great. Do you know who wrote the poem 'Happy Birthday to you, you live in a zoo, you look like a monkey, and you smell like one too'?
BOOKSELLER: . . .
CUSTOMER: Do they have their own collection?

♦

CUSTOMER: Do you have a crafts book on how to build a gun?

CUSTOMER: I've always thought I'd like to open up my own bookshop.
BOOKSELLER: Oh, really?
CUSTOMER: Yes, definitely. There's just something about it, you know? I just think it must be ever so relaxing.

♦

(phone rings)
BOOKSELLER: Hello?
CUSTOMER: Hi there. I have a complaint I'd like to make.
BOOKSELLER: I'm sorry to hear that; what seems to be the problem?
CUSTOMER: My daughter's been having nightmares about *The Gruffalo*.
BOOKSELLER: Right.
CUSTOMER: What are you going to do about it?
BOOKSELLER: Well, I hasten to add that I have never heard of a child having nightmares about *The Gruffalo* before. It's certainly not meant to be a scary book, and I'm sure the person who recommended this book to you didn't intend for this to happen either. When did you buy this book from us?
CUSTOMER: We didn't buy it from you.
BOOKSELLER: . . . Right.
CUSTOMER: I'm calling from Canada. I've googled all the bookshops I can find, and I'm calling you up to request that you stop stocking the book immediately.
BOOKSELLER: . . . Right.

(Pause)
CUSTOMER: So, are you going to get rid of the copies that you do have?
BOOKSELLER: No, I'm afraid we won't be doing that.
CUSTOMER: And why is that?
BOOKSELLER: Because this appears to be an isolated incident, and the book is loved by many of our customers.
CUSTOMER: Right . . . I see. Well. I'll be splitting my daughter's counselling bill and sharing it out amongst heartless booksellers like you!
BOOKSELLER: Out of interest, how many bookshops have agreed to get rid of the book so far?
CUSTOMER: I think you'll find that that's besides the point.
(Phone goes dead.)

♦

(Customer is reading a book from the shelf, pauses and folds the top of one of the pages over, then puts it back on the shelf)
BOOKSELLER: Excuse me, what are you doing?
CUSTOMER: I was just reading the first chapter of this book, but I'm going to be late meeting a friend for lunch. So, I'm just marking it and I'll finish reading it when I stop by tomorrow.

TALES FROM

Ripping Yarns

Ripping Yarns bookshop, opposite Highgate tube station in North London, is an antiquarian bookshop which has been around since the second world war. It was bought by Celia Mitchell and her husband, poet Adrian Mitchell, twenty seven years ago, and was reopened for them by Michael Palin and Terry Jones [of Monty Python fame]. Our bookshop dog is Daisy, a thirteen year old Golden Retriever who plonks herself in the middle of the shop and refuses to move if you want to get by.

www.rippingyarns.co.uk.

CUSTOMER: Excuse me, do you have any signed copies of Shakespeare plays?
BOOKSELLER: Er . . . do you mean signed by the people who performed the play?
CUSTOMER: No, I mean signed by William Shakespeare.
BOOKSELLER: . . .

♦

PERSON: Hi, I'm looking for a Mr. Patrick.
BOOKSELLER: No one of that name works here, sorry.
PERSON: But does he live here?
BOOKSELLER: . . . No one lives here; we're a bookshop.
PERSON: Are you sure?

♦

CUSTOMER: Hi, if I buy a book, read it, and bring it back, can I exchange it for another book?
BOOKSELLER: No . . . because then we wouldn't make any money.
CUSTOMER: Oh.

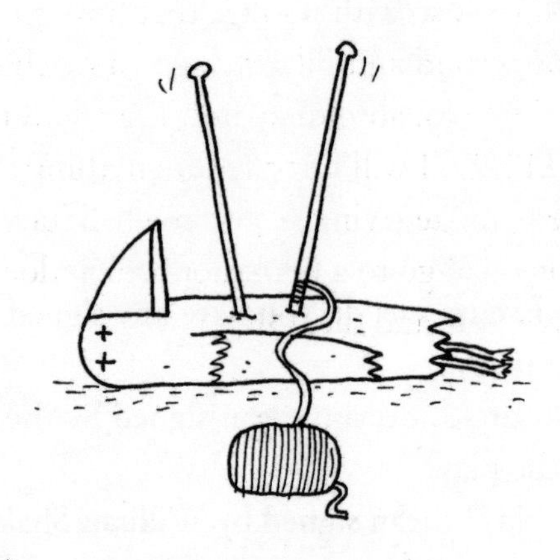

(on the phone)

BOOKSELLER: Hello, Ripping Yarns bookshop.

CUSTOMER: Do you have any mohair wool?

BOOKSELLER: Sorry, we're not a yarns shop, we're a bookshop.

CUSTOMER: You're called Ripping Yarns.

BOOKSELLER: Yes, that's 'yarns' as in stories.

CUSTOMER: Well, it's a stupid name.

BOOKSELLER: It's a Monty Python reference.

CUSTOMER: So you don't sell wool?

BOOKSELLER: No.

CUSTOMER: Hmf. That's ridiculous.

BOOKSELLER: . . . But we do sell dead parrots.

CUSTOMER: What?

BOOKSELLER: Parrots. Dead. Extinct. Expired. Would you like one?

CUSTOMER: Erm, no.

BOOKSELLER: OK, well, if you change your mind, do call back.

BOOKSELLER: OK, so with postage that brings your total to £13.05. One second and I'll get the card machine.
CUSTOMER: No. No, absolutely not. I demand that you charge me £12.99. I will not pay for anything that starts with thirteen. You're trying to give me bad luck. Now, change it, or I will go to a bookshop which doesn't want me to fall down a hole and die. OK?

♦

CUSTOMER: What kind of bookshop is this?
BOOKSELLER: We're an antiquarian bookshop.
CUSTOMER: Oh, so you sell books about fish.

♦

CUSTOMER: Do you sell ipod chargers?
BOOKSELLER: . . . No.
CUSTOMER: Why?

(phone rings)
BOOKSELLER: Hello, Ripping Yarns Bookshop
MAN: Hello, is that Ripping Yarns?
BOOKSELLER: Yes, it is.
MAN: The bookshop?
BOOKSELLER: . . . Yes.
MAN: Are you there?
BOOKSELLER: How do you mean?
MAN: I mean, are you at the shop now?
BOOKSELLER: Erm . . . yes, you just rang the number for the bookshop and I answered your call.

♦

CUSTOMER: Hello, I'd like a copy of *The Water Babies,* with nice illustrations. But I don't want to pay a lot of money for it, so could you show me what editions you do have so I can look at them, and then I can go and find one online?

♦

MAN: Hi, I've just self-published my art book. My friends tell me that I'm set to be the new Van Gogh. How many copies of my book would you like to pre-order?
BOOKSELLER: You know, Van Gogh was never appreciated in his lifetime.
MAN: . . .

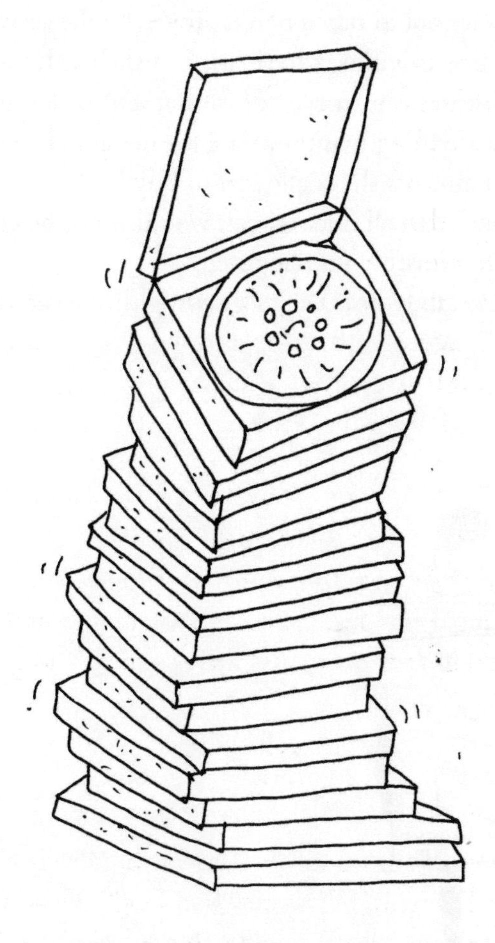

PIZZA DELIVERY MAN *(on entering the shop with a large pile of pizzas and seeing the bookseller, the only person in the bookshop)*: Hi, did you order fifteen pizzas?

WOMAN: Hi, my daughter is going to come by on her way home from school to buy a book. However, she seems to like to buy books with sex in them, and she's only twelve, so can I ask you to keep an eye out for her and make sure she doesn't buy anything inappropriate for her age? I can give you a list of authors she is allowed to buy.
BOOKSELLER: With all due respect, would it not be easier for you to come in with your daughter?
WOMAN: Certainly not. She's a grown girl; she can do it herself.

♦

CUSTOMER: I'd like to buy your heaviest book, please.

CUSTOMER: Do you have any books on the dark arts?
BOOKSELLER: . . . No.
CUSTOMER: Do you have any idea where I could find some?
BOOKSELLER: Why don't you try Knockturn Alley?
CUSTOMER: Where's that?
BOOKSELLER: Oh, the centre of London.
CUSTOMER: Thanks, I'll keep my eyes peeled for it.

♦

CUSTOMER: I tell you something, you must get some odd requests, working here.

♦

CUSTOMER: Did Beatrix Potter ever write a book about dinosaurs?

MAN: Do you have black and white film posters?
BOOKSELLER: Yes, we do. They're over here.
MAN: Do you have any posters of Adolf Hitler?
BOOKSELLER: Pardon?
MAN: Adolf Hitler.
BOOKSELLER: Well, he wasn't a film star, was he.
MAN: Yes, he was. He was American. Jewish, I think.
BOOKSELLER: . . .

♦

CUSTOMER *(poking his head through the door)*: Hi, can I bring my dog inside?
BOOKSELLER: Sure, there's a sign on the door that says that friendly dogs are allowed.
CUSTOMER: Well, she's not that friendly; she might bite people.
BOOKSELLER: . . . Well then please leave her outside.

♦

BOOKSELLER: Would you like a bag? We've got plastic and paper ones.
CUSTOMER: Well I would have asked for a bag, but you said 'plastic bag' not 'pla[r]stic bag', so now that you've said that, I don't want one.
BOOKSELLER: I'm not sure people say 'pla[r]stic bag.' Also, I'm from Newcastle so I say 'bath' not 'ba[r]th'.
CUSTOMER: Clearly you're uneducated.

(A customer in America ordered a 19th century book and, upon receiving it, said that it was in terrible condition. The booksellers were sure that the book had been accurately described, but said that the buyer could post the book back to them. The customer sent the book back in only a paper bag, with pieces of paper stuck to the pages that showed photographs. The spine was broken, as though he'd put said book on a photocopier, copied the images and posted the book back to the bookshop - never intending to keep it in the first place. The booksellers reported this to ABE books [the antiquarian bookselling website which the customer had bought the book through.]. They gave the booksellers the money to repair the book, and refunded the buyer with a strong warning.)

Several very rude emails ensued with choice phrases such as:

CUSTOMER: You will not forget this transaction. Every time an event goes wrong in your life, you will remember karma . . . I am a prophet and I bring you this message in the name of Jesus Christ.

A few weeks later, the customer posted an A4 envelope to the bookshop stuffed with pamphlets on how to recognise the devil within themselves.

CUSTOMER: I don't suppose I could have a cup of tea, could I?
BOOKSELLER: Well . . . erm . . .
CUSTOMER: Thanks, I'm parched.
BOOKSELLER *(indicating the bookshelves)*: Have you seen anything you'd like?
CUSTOMER: Oh, I'm not buying. I'm just waiting for my bus.

CUSTOMER *(holds up a biography):* Do you have this book but without the photographs?
BOOKSELLER: I think the photographs are published alongside the text in every edition.
CUSTOMER: Why?
BOOKSELLER: I suppose so you can see what everyone looked like.
CUSTOMER: I don't like photographs.
BOOKSELLER: OK.
CUSTOMER: Could you cut them out for me?
BOOKSELLER: . . .

CUSTOMER: Hi, do you have any new books?
BOOKSELLER: We're an antiquarian bookshop - our stock is made up of books which are out of print.
CUSTOMER: So other people have touched them?
BOOKSELLER: . . . Presumably, yes.
CUSTOMER: I don't think I'll bother, thanks.
BOOKSELLER: . . . OK.

CUSTOMER: Do you have any old porn magazines?

♦

CUSTOMER *(inclining her head)*: How are you guys doing?
BOOKSELLER: Oh, we're clinging on.
CUSTOMER: Oh you poor dears, it's this Kindle!
BOOKSELLER: Well, really, it's the supermarkets making people think that books aren't worth paying money for.
CUSTOMER: I hadn't thought of it like that. It is terrible, isn't it?
(*Five minutes later)*
CUSTOMER: How much is this book?
BOOKSELLER: That's £10.
CUSTOMER: Could I have it for £5?

CUSTOMER: There was a book in the eighties that I loved... but I can't remember the title.
BOOKSELLER: Can you remember anything about it?
CUSTOMER: I think it was called 360 fairy tales.
BOOKSELLER *(searches on British Library catalogue):* Nothing under that name, sorry.
CUSTOMER: I might have got the number wrong. Could you just type in 'fairy tales' and see what comes up?
BOOKSELLER: . . . That could take a while.

CUSTOMER: My dear, there's a long queue in the post office, and I only want a first class stamp. Do you have one I could buy from you?
BOOKSELLER: No, I'm sorry, I don't.
CUSTOMER: Well then, perhaps you could go and stand in the queue for me? You're a lot younger than myself; your legs can handle it.
BOOKSELLER: I'm afraid not - I'm running this bookshop by myself.
CUSTOMER: I'll keep an eye on it for you.
BOOKSELLER: No, I'm sorry, I'm afraid I can't do that; I'd get in a lot of trouble.
CUSTOMER: Well. You've been *extremely* unhelpful *(she storms out)*.

♦

CUSTOMER *(peering over)*: Do you have brown eyes?
BOOKSELLER: Yes, I do.
CUSTOMER: My mother told me never to trust anyone with brown eyes.
BOOKSELLER: . . . You have brown eyes.
CUSTOMER: . . .

♦

CUSTOMER: If I came to work here, would I get a discount at the off licence next door?

CUSTOMER: Hi there.
BOOKSELLER: Hi, can I help?
CUSTOMER: Yes, I was just admiring your shop sign outside.
BOOKSELLER: Thank you.
CUSTOMER: It's really lovely . . .
BOOKSELLER: . . . Yes.
CUSTOMER: . . . is it for sale?

MAN: Hi, I was wondering if I could ask you about a book I'm writing.
BOOKSELLER: Sure.
MAN: Well, it's here. *(He produces the 'book' - a series of things stuck into an A4 lined pad of paper)*
BOOKSELLER: Right, what's the premise?
MAN: It's a children's book. See, I've been taking pictures of stuff and my mate has been writing poems to go alongside it.
BOOKSELLER: OK. Are you a professional photographer?
MAN: No, I've just been taking photos of things on my mobile. They're pretty good though, yeah?
BOOKSELLER: Erm, well they're a little blurry.
MAN: Oh, that just makes them unique.
CUSTOMER: And your friend, has he had poems published elsewhere?
MAN: Nope, he doesn't believe in that kind of stuff.
BOOKSELLER: . . . OK . . . so what's your next step?
MAN: To get it published.
BOOKSELLER: What's your plan of action?
MAN: Just send it off to publishers.
BOOKSELLER: Which one?
MAN: Any old one. All of them. It ain't hard, is it?
BOOKSELLER: With all due respect, it is very hard.
MAN: Well our mates think it's a fantastic idea. And I don't think it can be hard - there are books everywhere these days – just look at this shop!
BOOKSELLER: Well, yes, but we are a *book*shop.

CUSTOMER: Do you have any books on star signs?
BOOKSELLER: Yes, our esoteric section is over here.
CUSTOMER: Good, thanks. It's just I really need to check mine – I have this overwhelming feeling that something bad is going to happen.

♦

CUSTOMER: I have *The Pickwick Papers*, first edition. How much will you buy it for?
BOOKSELLER *(examines book)*: Sorry, but this was was printed in 1910.
CUSTOMER: Yes.
BOOKSELLER: *The Pickwick Papers* was first printed in 1837; this isn't a first edition.
CUSTOMER: No, it was definitely first printed in 1910.
BOOKSELLER: Dickens was dead in 1910.
CUSTOMER: I don't think so. You're trying to con me.
BOOKSELLER: I promise you, I'm not.
CUSTOMER: *(glares for a while, then picks the book back up quickly)* I'm taking them to Sotheby's! *(storms out)*

CUSTOMER: Hi, do you have that sperm cookbook?
BOOKSELLER: No, we don't.
CUSTOMER: That's a shame; I really wanted to try it. Have you tried it?
BOOKSELLER: I have not.

CUSTOMER: Do you have a copy of Jane Eyre?
BOOKSELLER: Actually, I just sold that this morning, sorry!
CUSTOMER: Oh. Have you read it?
BOOKSELLER: Yes, it's one of my favourite books.
CUSTOMER: Oh, great *(sits down beside bookseller)*. Could you tell me all about it? I have to write an essay on it by tomorrow.

♦

CUSTOMER: Do you have a section on religion?
BOOKSELLER: Sure, it's just over here.
CUSTOMER: You've got Richard Dawkins's books on here next to copies of the Bible.
BOOKSELLER: That section is for all kinds of books relating to religion.
CUSTOMER: I hope you know that's a sin. And you will go to hell.

ELDERLY GENTLEMAN: Hello, do you have any books on sex?
BOOKSELLER: I think we have a couple, yes.
ELDERLY GENTLEMAN: Excellent. I've had a hip replacement, and I wasn't sure how long I had to wait, you see.
BOOKSELLER: . . . Right.
ELDERLY GENTLEMAN: I bet you could look it up on that computer there, though couldn't you?
BOOKSELLER: . . . I suppose I could, if I needed to.
ELDERLY GENTLEMAN: Excellent thing, the internet.

CUSTOMER: You have maps?
BOOKSELLER: Yes, we do. Road maps?
CUSTOMER: Yes.
BOOKSELLER: We have old ones - Ordnance Survey maps, and road maps, over here.
CUSTOMER: I need a map to Dover.
BOOKSELLER *(has a look)*: I'm not sure we have a specific south-east map. We have a road map of the UK, though, which has a map of the south-east in it.
CUSTOMER: No. I walk.
BOOKSELLER: You're walking?
CUSTOMER: Yes.
BOOKSELLER: To Dover?
CUSTOMER: Yes.
BOOKSELLER: That's very very far.
CUSTOMER: It's five miles, yes?
BOOKSELLER: No. It's about eighty miles.
CUSTOMER: You point me in the right direction?
BOOKSELLER: I don't know which way it is from here.
CUSTOMER: OK. I follow the smell of the sea.

♦

CUSTOMER: Do you have a copy of Mrs. Dalloway, but, like, really old – so from, like, 1850?
BOOKSELLER: . . .

Dear Sirs,

I am writing to see if you have any positions available at your bookshop. I really love your shop, and the personalised service I get from you when I've been in previously. Your shop is one dear to my heart.

I have attached my CV.

Best.

(Someone who CC'd this email to every bookshop in North London).

♦

(Man enters bookshop smoking a cigarette)
BOOKSELLER: Excuse me?
MAN: Yes?
BOOKSELLER: Could you put that cigarette out, please?
MAN: Why?
BOOKSELLER: Because it's illegal to smoke in a public place.
MAN: This isn't a public place; there's only you and me here.
BOOKSELLER: Yes, well, it's still a public place. And, apart from anything else, this shop is rather flammable.
MAN: Why?
BOOKSELLER: . . . because it's filled with paper.
MAN: Is it?

CUSTOMER: Do you have a nature section? I'm looking for a nature guide, you know, for places to go.
BOOKSELLER: Sure, our nature section is just down here.
CUSTOMER: No, sorry, not nature – naturist.
BOOKSELLER: Oh!

CUSTOMER: Did I leave my bicycle in here?

♦

CUSTOMER *(to their friend)*: God, the *Famous Five* titles really were crap, weren't they? *Five Go Camping. Five Go Off in a Caravan....* If it was *Five Go Down To a Crack House* it might be a bit more exciting.

♦

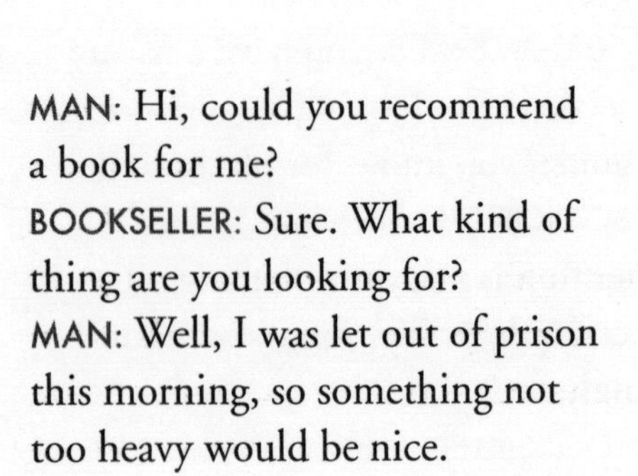

MAN: Hi, could you recommend a book for me?
BOOKSELLER: Sure. What kind of thing are you looking for?
MAN: Well, I was let out of prison this morning, so something not too heavy would be nice.

CUSTOMER: (*on noticing Nicola Morgan's 'Write to be Published' advertisement in front of the desk*): A book on how to get published?
BOOKSELLER: Yes. Nicola's fabulous.
CUSTOMER: Is it about self-publishing?
BOOKSELLER: Nicola focuses mainly on mainstream publishing.
CUSTOMER: Oh, I've written that kind of book myself.
BOOKSELLER: Have you?
CUSTOMER: Yeah. I self-publish my own novels, and I self-published this book on getting published the traditional way. I don't have experience of it, but I thought I'd give it a go. It hasn't sold as well as I thought it would.

♦

CUSTOMER: Oh wow, this shop is lovely!
BOOKSELLER: Thank you.
CUSTOMER: I was in a bakery just like it the other day.
BOOKSELLER: . . .

♦

CUSTOMER: Do you bother to arrange your books at all, or are they just plonked places?
BOOKSELLER: They're in alphabetical order...
CUSTOMER: Oh.

(Phone rings)
BOOKSELLER: Hello?
PERSON: Hi there, can I speak to the manager of the property?
BOOKSELLER: Speaking. How can I help?
PERSON: I'm calling to see if you'd be interested in stocking some cleaning products in your vicinity.
BOOKSELLER: To sell?
PERSON: Yes.
BOOKSELLER: We're a bookshop.
PERSON: Yes. Could you see yourselves branching out into this area?
BOOKSELLER: Not really, no.
PERSON: How about I send over a sample of products and you can see how you get on?
BOOKSELLER: No, thank you.
PERSON: Books and cleaning products work well together.
BOOKSELLER: Do they?
PERSON: I'm sure we could make this work.
BOOKSELLER: No, thank you.
PERSON: I think you're missing out on a very interesting opportunity. Can you think of any other bookshops who might be interested?

♦

CUSTOMER: Do you stock Nigella Lawson under 'Sex' or 'Cookery'?
BOOKSELLER: It's a tough call, isn't it?

CUSTOMER: If I give you these three paperbacks, will you sell them and give the money to charity?
BOOKSELLER: We're not a charity bookshop.
CUSTOMER: Oh. Where does your money go to?
BOOKSELLER: . . . It goes into keeping us in business.

♦

CUSTOMER: Some of these books are dusty . . . can't you hoover them?

CUSTOMER: OK, so you want this book?
THEIR DAUGHTER: Yes!
CUSTOMER: *Peter Pan*?
THEIR DAUGHTER: Yes, please. Because he can fly.
CUSTOMER: Yes, he can – he's very good at flying.
THEIR DAUGHTER: Why can't I fly, daddy?
CUSTOMER: Because of evolution, sweetheart.

♦

CUSTOMER: Do you have a book on how to breathe underwater?
BOOKSELLER: You mean Julie Orringer's short story collection: '*How to Breathe Underwater*'?
CUSTOMER: Is that fact?
BOOKSELLER: No, it's fiction – the title's a metaphor.
CUSTOMER: . . . Oh. No. I need a book on how to actually breathe underwater.
BOOKSELLER: . . .

CUSTOMER: Hi.
BOOKSELLER: Hi there, how can I help?
CUSTOMER: Could you please explain Kindle to me.
BOOKSELLER: Sure. It's an e-reader, which means you download books and read them on a small hand-held computer.
CUSTOMER: Oh OK, I see. So . . . this Kindle. Are the books on that paperback or hardback?

♦

CUSTOMER *(poking her head around the door, glancing at our six by six metre bookshop)*: Do you have a café in here?
BOOKSELLER: No, I'm afraid we don't.
CUSTOMER: Oh, I was looking for a bookshop with a café.
BOOKSELLER: If you want a cup of tea, there's a café four doors down.
CUSTOMER: Could I take some books there with me to look through and browse? And then bring them back?

CUSTOMER: Do you have any old copies of Dickens?
BOOKSELLER: We've got a copy of *David Copperfield* from 1850 for £100.
CUSTOMER: Why is it so expensive if it's that old?

(A man is walking around the shop, carrying a plastic bag stuffed with Nike jackets)
MAN *(to a customer)*: Would you like to buy a Nike jacket?
CUSTOMER: Erm, no.
MAN: *(to another person)*: Can I interest you in a Nike jacket? Genuine Nike.
BOOKSELLER: Excuse me, what are you doing?
MAN: I was just seeing if anyone would like to buy a jacket.
BOOKSELLER: Please don't bother my customers.
MAN: But it's a shop . . . they're here to buy things.

CUSTOMER: This book has a couple of tears to some of the pages.
BOOKSELLER: Yes, unfortunately some of the older books have some wear and tear from previous owners.
CUSTOMER: So, will you lower the price? It says here it's £20.
BOOKSELLER: I'm sorry but we take into account the condition of the books when we price them; if that book was in a better condition, it would be worth a lot more than £20.
CUSTOMER: Well, you can't have taken this tear here into account *(points to page)* or this one here *(points to another page),* because my son did those two minutes ago.
BOOKSELLER: So, the book is now more damaged than it was before, because of your son?
CUSTOMER: Yes. Exactly. So now will you lower the price?

CUSTOMER: Do you do gift wrap?
BOOKSELLER: No, I'm afraid we don't, sorry.
CUSTOMER: I tell you what; I'll nip to the Post Office and buy some wrapping paper. Then I'll bring it back and you can wrap the book up for me, ok? You're a shop, for Christ's sake, you're here to offer me a service.

♦

CUSTOMER: Do you have a book on dinosaurs? My grandson's really into them.
BOOKSELLER: Absolutely, we have one over here.
CUSTOMER: Does it have every type in here?
BOOKSELLER: I believe it's a very comprehensive collection, yes.
CUSTOMER: Great. So, does it have a chapter on dragons?

♦

CUSTOMER: Do you have any old Elvis CDs?
BOOKSELLER: No, we don't sell music, sorry. We might have a book on Elvis, though.
CUSTOMER: Would any of those come with a life-size cut-out of him?
BOOKSELLER: . . . I doubt it, no.

Everything in
moderation.

CUSTOMER: Wow, you have a whole bookcase of Enid Blyton?
BOOKSELLER: Yep, we do. *Famous Five, Secret Seven, Five Find Outers, Noddy* – all of it there.
CUSTOMER: I loved the *Famous Five* when I was younger.
BOOKSELLER: Yes, they were fun.
CUSTOMER: I'm so glad you think so. I know that there are a lot of people who say that Anne was stupid and that she shouldn't have just been doing the 'girly' things, and that it was offensive.
BOOKSELLER: Well . . .
CUSTOMER: I think all this political correctness has just gone way too far. I mean, who cares that Enid Blyton openly said that a woman should be the one to do the cooking and the cleaning? So she should.
BOOKSELLER: Well—
CUSTOMER: – and then there are those who complain about the *Noddy* picture books, you know?
BOOKSELLER: Hmmm.
CUSTOMER: Well, I say that a bit of racism never hurt anyone.
BOOKSELLER: . . .
CUSTOMER: Everything in moderation, don't you agree?

♦

CUSTOMER: Do you have a book that has a list of aphrodisiacs? I've got a date on Friday.

CUSTOMER: *(Drops an old, expensive book on the floor by accident)*: Great shot!
BOOKSELLER: *(glares)*
CUSTOMER: I mean . . . sorry.

CUSTOMER: Oh, look, they've got a section on dictionaries. Perhaps we should get your brother one for school, for Spanish, what do you think?
HER DAUGHTER: Can we get one for when we go to Scotland for our holidays?
CUSTOMER: They talk English in Scotland, too, sweetie.

(Phone rings)
BOOKSELLER: Hello, Ripping Yarns bookshop.
CUSTOMER: Hello, I've got some books I'd like to sell.
BOOKSELLER: Sure. What kinds of books do you have?
CUSTOMER: Oh, boxes and boxes of stuff. I've got some children's books, some comics, some old magazines and newspapers, an exercise bike, a couple of art books and some cookery books, too.
BOOKSELLER: What was the one in the middle?
CUSTOMER: Erm. Old magazines.
BOOKSELLER: No, the one after that.
CUSTOMER: An exercise bike.
BOOKSELLER: Yes . . . we won't be wanting the exercise bike.

CUSTOMER: Do you have a, er . . . a back room?
BOOKSELLER: You mean a store room?
CUSTOMER: Ah, a store room. OK. Yes.
BOOKSELLER: Yes, we have a store room . . .
CUSTOMER: I'd like to *(wink)* buy something *(wink)* from your store room.
BOOKSELLER: Excuse me?
CUSTOMER: Oh, right, you've got a buzz word, haven't you? A password?
BOOKSELLER: I think you're mistaken. I think you're thinking of somewhere else.
CUSTOMER: Oh. Really?
BOOKSELLER: Yes. I think you should leave now.
CUSTOMER: Oh. *(moves away)*
(Customer comes back two minutes later)
CUSTOMER: Just to clarify, I was asking for drugs and you were saying you're not that kind of place, right?
BOOKSELLER: That's right.
CUSTOMER: OK, thanks.
Pause
CUSTOMER: Could you recommend—
BOOKSELLER: No.
CUSTOMER: OK, OK . . . Thanks.
BOOKSELLER: You're welcome.
CUSTOMER: Bye, then.
BOOKSELLER: Goodbye.
CUSTOMER: Very nice bookshop.
BOOKSELLER: Thank you.

CUSTOMER: What's your name?
BOOKSELLER: Jen.
CUSTOMER: Hmmm. I don't like that name. Is it ok if I call you something else?

♦

CUSTOMER: Someone should have taught that Shakespeare guy how to spell. I mean, am I right, or am I right?

CUSTOMER: Do you have security cameras in here?
BOOKSELLER: Yes.
CUSTOMER: Oh. *(customer slides a book out from inside his jacket and places it back on the shelf)*

CUSTOMER *(holding up a magazine from the sixties)*: It says on the front cover that this magazine was supposed to come with half a jigsaw puzzle, but you don't have the jigsaw puzzle. Does that mean I can have the magazine for free?

CUSTOMER: Do you have *Dr Who and the Secrets of the Hidden Planet of Time*?
BOOKSELLER: I'm not familiar with that one. Hang on and I'll check our system for you.
CUSTOMER: Thank you.
BOOKSELLER: I'm afraid I can't find it on our database, or on the British Library catalogue. Are you sure you've got the right title?
CUSTOMER: No, not at all. I don't know that it actually exists.
BOOKSELLER: . . . what do you mean?
CUSTOMER: Oh, I was just driving to work yesterday and I thought up the title and I thought 'now *that* sounds like the kind of book I'd like to read', you know?
BOOKSELLER: Hmmm. Well, I'm afraid you can't read it, as it hasn't been written.
CUSTOMER: Never mind, never mind – just thought I'd check.
BOOKSELLER: We do have lots of other *Dr. Who* novels over here, though, if you'd like to take a look.
CUSTOMER: No, it's ok. I'll go home and have another think and come back again.

BOOKSELLER: Hi, can I help you at all?
CUSTOMER: I don't give a damn about books – they bore me.
BOOKSELLER: I'm not sure you're in the right place, then.
CUSTOMER: No, I am. I just wanted to ask what specific colour you painted your bookshelves? I love this colour. I mean, the right colour can make books look more appealing, can't it?
BOOKSELLER: Can it?
CUSTOMER: And the smell of the paint takes away the smell of the books, too. Which is also a plus.

CUSTOMER: Hi, my best friend came in last weekend and bought a book, and she really loved it. Do you have another copy?
BOOKSELLER: What was the title?
CUSTOMER: Oh, right. Yeah. I don't remember.

CUSTOMER: Do you have a copy of Bella Swan's favourite book? You know, from *Twilight*?

(Bookseller sighs and pulls a copy of Wuthering Heights off the shelf)

CUSTOMER: Do you have the one with the cover that looks like *Twilight*?

BOOKSELLER: No. This is an antiquarian bookshop, so this is an old edition of the book.

CUSTOMER: But it's still the one with that girl Cathy and the dangerous guy, right?

BOOKSELLER: Yes, it's still the story by Emily Bronte.

CUSTOMER: Right. Do you think they'll make it into a film?

BOOKSELLER: They've made several films of it. The one where Ralph Fiennes plays Heathcliff is very good.

CUSTOMER: What? Voldemort plays Heathcliff?

BOOKSELLER: Well . . .

CUSTOMER: But that's Edward's role.

BOOKSELLER: *Wuthering Heights* was written well before both *Harry Potter* and *Twilight*.

CUSTOMER: Yeah, but Voldemort killed Cedric, who's played by Robert Pattinson, and now Voldemort's playing Edward's role in *Wuthering Heights,* because Edward's character is Heathcliff. I think that Emily Bronte's trying to say something about vampires.

BOOKSELLER: . . . that's £8.

CUSTOMER: For what?

BOOKSELLER: For the book.

CUSTOMER: Oh, no, it's OK, I'm going to go and try and find the Voldemort DVD version.

CUSTOMER: I've got a while before my bus. Are you and any of the other customers interested in playing cards?

CUSTOMER: Do you have any piano sheet music, but for guitars?
BOOKSELLER: You mean, do I have sheet music for guitars?
CUSTOMER: Yes.

CUSTOMER: Have you read every single book in here?
BOOKSELLER: No, I can't say I have.
CUSTOMER: Well you're not very good at your job, are you?

CUSTOMER: I'm looking for that famous book – you know, the Disney one, where Donald Duck is an accountant.

CUSTOMER: Do you have an easy version of *Moonlight Sonata* for piano?
BOOKSELLER: We have box of sheet music by the music books section. I'll have a look.
CUSTOMER: Thanks.
BOOKSELLER: Yep. Here's a *Moonlight Sonata* for grade two.
CUSTOMER: And that's easy?
BOOKSELLER: Compared to the real thing, yes.
CUSTOMER: So, I should be able to play it, yeah?
BOOKSELLER: I don't know. How long have you been playing?
CUSTOMER: Oh, I don't know how to play, I thought I'd just try.
BOOKSELLER: Right. Can you read sheet music?
CUSTOMER: Well . . . sure . . . it's just the alphabet, isn't it?

♦

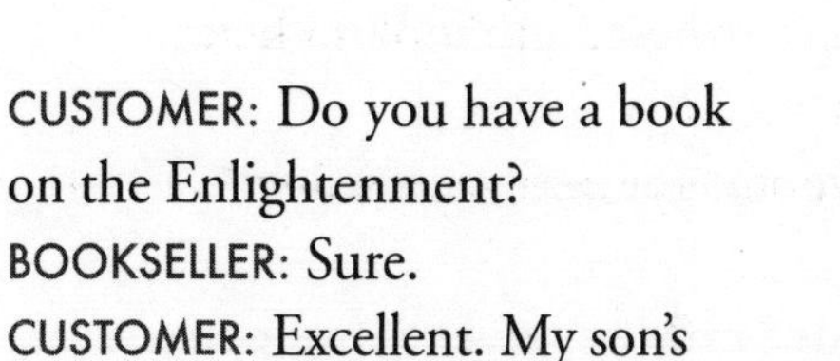

CUSTOMER: Do you have a book on the Enlightenment?
BOOKSELLER: Sure.
CUSTOMER: Excellent. My son's just about to start studying it at school. It's all about the light bulb being invented, right?

CUSTOMER: Oh, sorry. I thought you were the Post Office.... You're not, are you?

♦

MAN: *(bursting through the bookshop door)* Oi! Could you keep it down? We're trying to film something outside.
BOOKSELLER: . . . I'm not making any noise.
MAN: Well, it looked like you were about to.
BOOKSELLER: . . . It's just me and the books here; we're not going to have a raucous party.
MAN: Yeah, well, just make sure you don't.

♦

CUSTOMER: I've got some books I'd like to sell *(plonks them on the desk)*. I'd like twenty five quid for the lot.
BOOKSELLER: Didn't you buy these from us last week?
CUSTOMER: Yes.
BOOKSELLER: I see they've still got our prices in.
CUSTOMER: Uh-huh.
BOOKSELLER: . . . You didn't even pay twenty five pounds for these in the first place.
CUSTOMER: Yes, but they're older now than they were last week, see. So they must be worth more.

BOOKSELLER: Hi, can I help?
CUSTOMER: Yes. I've got a copy of *The Secrets of Houdini* that I'd like to sell. It's very rare. And it's signed by Houdini himself.
BOOKSELLER: Actually signed by Houdini?
CUSTOMER: Yes. *(hands book over)*
BOOKSELLER: Ah *(upon noticing signature to frontispiece),* I'm pretty sure that this signature is actually part of the printing.
CUSTOMER: Why?
BOOKSELLER: Because the date next to the signature is 1924.
CUSTOMER: So?
BOOKSELLER: Well, this book was printed in 1932.
CUSTOMER: Perhaps the date on the signature actually reads 1934.
BOOKSELLER: In that case, the signature is fake.
CUSTOMER: Why?
BOOKSELLER: Because Houdini died in 1926.
CUSTOMER: But if you feel the signature, you can tell that it's ridged. It doesn't feel like the rest of the page.
BOOKSELLER: Yes, I see what you mean, it's almost like someone's gone over it with a pencil, isn't it?
CUSTOMER *(frowning)*: That is a *genuine* Houdini signature.
BOOKSELLER: I assure you; it's part of the printing.
CUSTOMER: He signed the book himself.
BOOKSELLER: And dated it 1924? In a book published in 1932? Six years after he died?
CUSTOMER: . . . Perhaps it was his last unsolvable act of magic.
BOOKSELLER: Unfortunately I don't think that Houdini's last cryptic trick was to come back from the dead, sign your book, and make you a whole lot of money.

In June
CUSTOMER: When's the London Book Fair?
BOOKSELLER: It was on in April.
CUSTOMER: So . . . it's not on right now, then?

♦

CUSTOMER: You must get so much time to read, just sitting here surrounded by books.
BOOKSELLER: What is it you do?
CUSTOMER: Me? I work in a clothes shop.
BOOKSELLER: Well, you must get so much time to try clothes on, just standing there, surrounded by clothes.

♦

CUSTOMER: I'm looking for a book about this big *(indicates size)*. I've got a space on my bookshelf and I need to fill it. It's really bugging me.
BOOKSELLER: What kind of book would you like?
CUSTOMER: I don't care, just as long as it's this exact size.

CUSTOMER: Do you have any second hand crosswords?
BOOKSELLER: You mean crosswords that have already been filled in?
CUSTOMER: Yes. I love crosswords, but they're ever so difficult.

CUSTOMER: Which way is it to Highgate cemetery?
(Bookseller hands over a map)
CUSTOMER: Thanks. And that vampire that used to live there... he's dead now, right?

(On putting the key in the door of the bookshop to open up in the morning, a customer comes up)
BOOKSELLER: Excuse me, sorry, I'm afraid I'm not open yet. If you could wait two seconds and I'll get the boxes out of the way and put the lights on.
CUSTOMER: Oh, don't worry, I'll only be a second. *(Barges past into bookshop)*

♦

CUSTOMER: I've got some books to sell.
BOOKSELLER: Hi, thanks. I'm just serving some customers at the moment. Could you join the back of the queue?
CUSTOMER: Er, I'm selling you books, I'm here for *your* benefit.
BOOKSELLER: These other people are here to buy books, they are also here for the shop's benefit.
CUSTOMER: You've got thirty seconds to buy them, or I'm leaving. You need to learn to prioritise.

♦

CUSTOMER *(to her friend, upon opening a copy of The Lord of the Rings)*: Oh, look, this one's got a map in the front.
CUSTOMER'S FRIEND: Oh yeah. Where's it of?
CUSTOMER: Mor... Mor-dor.
CUSTOMER'S FRIEND: Oh. Where's that then?

CUSTOMER: Hi, I just wanted to check: are you a bookshop, or are you a library?
BOOKSELLER: . . . We're a bookshop.
CUSTOMER: You should probably have a sign saying that somewhere; it's confusing.
BOOKSELLER: We have a big sign outside that says 'Ripping Yarns Bookshop.'
CUSTOMER: Yes, well, that's ambivalent, isn't it?
BOOKSELLER: It is?

♦

CUSTOMER: Who wrote the Bible? I can't remember.
CUSTOMER'S FRIEND: Jesus.

CUSTOMER: It's amazing, isn't it, how little we really know about writers' lives? Especially the old ones.
BOOKSELLER: I guess the lives of writers have changed a lot.
CUSTOMER: Yes. And don't forget about those women who used to write under male names.
BOOKSELLER: Yes, like George Eliot.
CUSTOMER: I always thought Charles Dickens was probably a woman.
BOOKSELLER: . . . I'm pretty sure Charles Dickens was a man.
CUSTOMER: But who's to say?
BOOKSELLER: Well, he was pretty prominent in society; lots of people saw him.
CUSTOMER: But maybe that was all a show – maybe that was her brother, whilst *Charlene* was at home, writing.
BOOKSELLER: . . .

CUSTOMER: I've forgotten my glasses, could you read the beginning of this book to me to see if I like it?

♦

(Bookseller puts book that the customer has bought into a paper bag)
CUSTOMER: Don't you have a plastic bag? I'm sick of all this recycling nonsense. It's not doing any of us any good.

♦

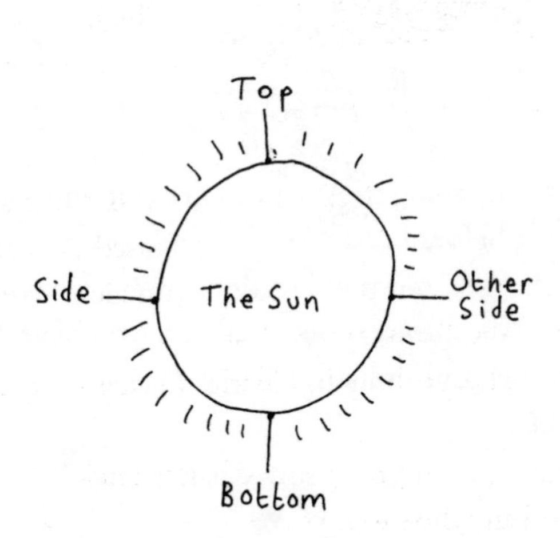

CUSTOMER: Where do you keep your maps?
BOOKSELLER: Over here, what kind of map are you looking for? A county, the UK, Europe, a world map?
CUSTOMER: I want a map of the sun.

CUSTOMER: Is your poetry section split up into rhyming and non-rhyming sections?
BOOKSELLER: No, it's just in alphabetical order. What kind of poetry are you looking for?
CUSTOMER: Rhyming. Preferably iambic pentameter, in poems of no more than ten lines, by a female poet. But, other than that, I don't mind.

♦

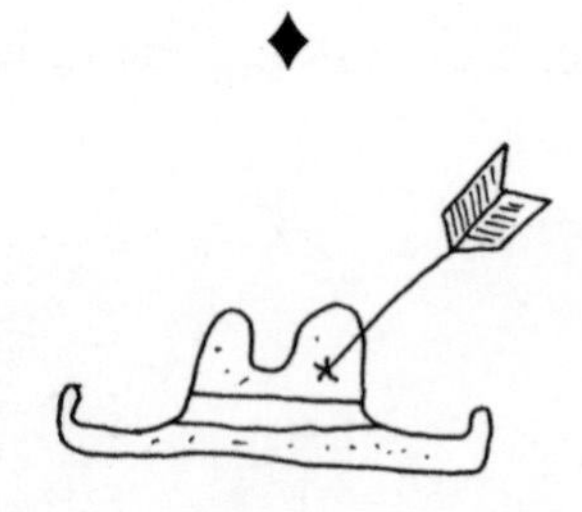

CUSTOMER: I'm going to America next year and I'd like to read about it before I go.
BOOKSELLER: Sure, our travel section's probably your best bet.
CUSTOMER: No, I don't think so . . . Do you have any stories about cowboys and Indians?
BOOKSELLER: . . .

CUSTOMER: You don't have a very good selection of books.
BOOKSELLER: We've got over ten thousand books.
CUSTOMER: Well, you don't have the book I've written!
(Storms out)

(Phone rings)
BOOKSELLER: Hello, Ripping Yarns bookshop.
CUSTOMER: Hi there. If I buy a book and pay for it over the phone, could you bring it over the road to my house? I just live round the corner.
BOOKSELLER: Are you unable to leave your house?
CUSTOMER: Well, no . . . but it's raining.

♦

CUSTOMER: Do you have that Enid Blyton series? Not the *Secret Seven* – the other one.
BOOKSELLER: *The Five Find Outers*? *The Famous Five*?
CUSTOMER: Yes, *The Famous Five,* that's the one. The one with the transsexual.

CUSTOMER: You should consider arranging your books by size and colour.
BOOKSELLER: But then no one would be able to find anything.
CUSTOMER: Well, that doesn't matter. It'd look pretty.

♦

CUSTOMER: Do you have the time?
BOOKSELLER: Yes. It's just after four o'clock.
CUSTOMER: No, it isn't.

♦

CUSTOMER: Hi, I've got a book on reserve and I've come to pick it up.
BOOKSELLER: Sure, what's your name, and what was the title of the book?
CUSTOMER: My name's Stuart and it was volume one of *The Waverley Children's Dictionary.*
BOOKSELLER: I'm sorry, I can't see that on our reserve shelf. When did you come in and reserve it?
CUSTOMER: Oh, it was a fair while ago now.
BOOKSELLER: A couple of weeks?
CUSTOMER: No . . . more like a year and a half.
BOOKSELLER: I'm afraid we only reserve books for a month and then they have to go back out in the shop. We don't have the space to keep them to one side for longer.
CUSTOMER: But I was really looking forward to reading that!

CUSTOMER: Hi, do you sell Christmas trees?
BOOKSELLER: No . . .
CUSTOMER: Oh. I thought it was worth asking because you've got lots of Christmas books in the window.

♦

CUSTOMER: Who do I speak to about me selling you some books?
BOOKSELLER: That would be me.
CUSTOMER: Where's your boss? Is he not here?
BOOKSELLER: The owner of the shop isn't here, she's at home.
CUSTOMER: And who's her boss? What's his name?
BOOKSELLER: She *is* the boss.
CUSTOMER: Oh. Well you're all modern, aren't you?

♦

CUSTOMER: Do you have any of those books where you can change the names of the main character to the name of the person you're giving the book to? Do you have *Alice in Wonderland,* but not Alice, I'd like *Sarah in Wonderland*.
BOOKSELLER: I'm afraid you have to buy those from the publisher, as they're a print on demand service.
CUSTOMER: Yeah, I don't really have time to do that. Do you have a copy of *Alice*? Then I can buy some Tipp-ex or something, and edit it.

CUSTOMER *(holding up a copy of Ulysses)*: Why is this book so long? Isn't it supposed to be set in one day only? How can this many pages of things happen to one person in one day? I mean, I get up, have breakfast, go to work, come home... sometimes I might go out for a drink, and that's it! And, I mean, that doesn't fill a book, does it?

♦

CUSTOMER: Do you have any jobs going?
BOOKSELLER: Have you worked in a bookshop before?
CUSTOMER: No.
BOOKSELLER: I take it you enjoy reading?
CUSTOMER: No, I don't read at all.
BOOKSELLER: So... why do you want to work in a bookshop?
CUSTOMER: Well, I don't really. It's just that I've moved into a flat up the street, and I'd like a job within walking distance.

CUSTOMER: Where do you keep *Hamlet*? You know 'to be or not to be'? Is it in philosophy?

CUSTOMER: Is your mother around?
BOOKSELLER: . . . I run this bookshop.
CUSTOMER: Oh. Sorry.

(Phone rings)
BOOKSELLER: Hello, Ripping Yarns bookshop.
CUSTOMER: Hi. My friend recommended you to me. She said you sell the most amazing knee high socks.
BOOKSELLER: We don't sell socks, we're a bookshop.
CUSTOMER: Oh, have you sold out?
BOOKSELLER: Of what?
CUSTOMER: Of socks.
BOOKSELLER: No, we're a *book*shop.
CUSTOMER: Oh, OK.

♦

CUSTOMER *(speaking loudly on her mobile)*: Why aren't you *here* yet? I don't like walking around with two thousand pounds in cash on me! Hurry up and pick me up!

(Customer's phone rings)
OTHER CUSTOMER: Will you turn that off? There are laws about mobile phones in bookshops, you know.

♦

CUSTOMER: Do you have a restricted section?

♦

CUSTOMER: Is this Hampstead Heath?
BOOKSELLER: No, it's a bookshop.

(Customer walks in and leaves the door wide open)
OTHER CUSTOMER: Could you close that door behind you?
CUSTOMER: I'm just paying for this book, and then I'm leaving again. I'll only be two seconds.
OTHER CUSTOMER: You've already been in here ten seconds and now it's freezing in here.
CUSTOMER: That's because you're blocking my way to the till!
OTHER CUSTOMER: Just close the bloody door. Where are your manners? This is a bookshop!

CUSTOMER: You know, I'm not sure I've ever really read a whole book before...

CUSTOMER: I've been looking through your geography section – I can't find any books on Atlantis.
BOOKSELLER: You know, I think we managed to lose those.

CUSTOMER: You know, if you put boxes of books outside you'd attract a lot more customers.
BOOKSELLER: . . . it's snowing outside right now.

♦

CUSTOMER: Do you have Philip Pullman's *The Book of Dust?*
BOOKSELLER: No, I don't think a publication date has even been set for that book yet.
CUSTOMER: I know, it's just I thought you might already have a copy, considering you're an antiquarian bookshop.
BOOKSELLER: . . . Antiquarian means old. We don't have books, you know, from the future.
CUSTOMER: Ah.

CUSTOMER: Do you have any comics where the women have really big breasts? It's . . . er . . . it's for an art project.

CUSTOMER: Do you have Agatha Christie's *Death in Denial*?

CUSTOMER *(holding up a book about knitting)* Do you think I could knit using my own hair?

CUSTOMER: I'd love to hold a fashion photo shoot in here. We could get models to come in and half bury themselves in books on the floor, or get them to hang from the bookshelves. Do you think your customers would mind?

CUSTOMER: What books could I buy to make guests look at my bookshelf and think: 'Wow, that guy's intelligent'?

CUSTOMER: We've got so many books at home that we've had to start recycling them.
BOOKSELLER: You mean you're taking them to charity shops?
CUSTOMER: No, I mean we've actually started recycling them. You know, putting them out with the bins.
BOOKSELLER: . . .

♦

CUSTOMER: Can books conduct electricity?

CUSTOMER: Who wrote *Winnie the Pooh*?
BOOKSELLER: A. A. Milne.
CUSTOMER: Ah, yes, that's right. She hasn't brought out anything new in a while, has she?
BOOKSELLER: No, you're right, he hasn't.

CUSTOMER: Do you have any *Robin Hood* stories where he doesn't steal from the rich? My husband's called Robin and I'd like to buy him a copy for his birthday, but he's a banker, so ...

CUSTOMER: Do you have any old knitting patterns?
BOOKSELLER: We do, as it happens, yes. They're over here.
CUSTOMER: And do you sell knitting needles?
BOOKSELLER: No, I'm afraid not.
CUSTOMER: But I'll need those when using the old knitting patterns.
BOOKSELLER: Well . . .
CUSTOMER: And do you sell wool?
BOOKSELLER: No, just the knitting patterns and magazines.
CUSTOMER: You haven't thought this through properly, have you? How am I supposed to knit a scarf without knitting needles and wool?
BOOKSELLER: You're going to have to buy those things from another shop, I'm afraid.
CUSTOMER: It would be much better for me if I could buy everything in one place.
BOOKSELLER: Unfortunately we can't stock everything relevant to the books we have, otherwise we'd be full of gardening tools, sewing machines, cooking ingredients and paint brushes.
CUSTOMER: What are you talking about? I don't need any of those things. I only need wool and knitting needles. I'm not going to knit with a paintbrush!

CUSTOMER: I've always wondered how one writes a book.
BOOKSELLER: How do you mean?
CUSTOMER: I mean, how did authors do it before computers were invented?
BOOKSELLER: Well, there were typewriters and, before that, they wrote by hand.
CUSTOMER: You would have thought they could have invented computers faster to make writers' lives easier.
BOOKSELLER: . . . yes.
CUSTOMER: And then, now that they have computers, is there a program that they use?
BOOKSELLER: A program?
CUSTOMER: A computer program that you know, puts everything in the right order. Tells you what to name your characters and things.
BOOKSELLER: No, I don't think so. Well, I'm sure that there are programs with guidelines but I don't think people tend to use them. They just write.
CUSTOMER: They just write?
BOOKSELLER: Yes, they just write the story they want to tell.
CUSTOMER: So they just use something like Word?
BOOKSELLER: Yes, I guess so.
CUSTOMER: But, you see, that's what I really don't understand.
BOOKSELLER: What?
CUSTOMER: Well Word documents are A4 size, and a book is never that big. It's a lot smaller.
BOOKSELLER: . . .
CUSTOMER: So, how on earth do they get it all to fit?
BOOKSELLER: . . .

CUSTOMER: Do you have any books on Japan?
BOOKSELLER: Sure. A travel guide or a history?
CUSTOMER: Yes.
BOOKSELLER: Which one?
CUSTOMER: Both.
BOOKSELLER: Right.
CUSTOMER: . . . And it should also have stories for children.
BOOKSELLER: . . .
CUSTOMER: Illustrated.
BOOKSELLER: . . .
CUSTOMER: And it has to be a hardback, not a paperback. And it should be a good price.
BOOKSELLER: . . .
CUSTOMER: A really nice old edition, with a modern twist.
BOOKSELLER: . . . I'm really not sure what kind of book you're looking for.

WEIRD THINGS CUSTOMERS SAY IN

other bookshops

CUSTOMER: Do you sell reading books?
BOOKSELLER: Errr . . .
CUSTOMER: You know, books you can read?
BOOKSELLER: Did you have anything in mind? Fiction? Biography? Any other subject?
CUSTOMER: Just reading.
BOOKSELLER: Oh, sorry, do you mean books on learning how to read? My mistake. Yes, I can show you . . .
CUSTOMER *(interrupts)*: NO! I JUST WANT A BOOK TO READ!
BOOKSELLER: . . .

♦

CUSTOMER: I'm always on night shift at work.
BOOKSELLER *(jokingly)*: Is that why you're buying so many vampire novels?
CUSTOMER *(seriously)*: You can never be too prepared.

Lauretta Nagel: *Constellation Books, Reisterstown, Maryland, USA.*

CUSTOMER: I've just been to the funeral parlour to make arrangements should anything happen to me, and to give them my directions for the service. Can I have my funeral service in your shop?
BOOKSELLER *(nervous giggle)*: Well, I um . . . you're not serious are you?
CUSTOMER: Well, it would be just wonderful wouldn't it . . . I mean, not the furnace part, obviously, but the service.
BOOKSELLER: Erm . . .

Sam Barnes: *Books and Ink Bookshop, Banbury, UK.*

♦

MAN: *(sidles up to counter and whispers)*: Hi . . .
BOOKSELLER: Hello?
MAN: Do you sell condoms?
BOOKSELLER: . . . Sorry, no, this is a bookshop.
MAN: Oh . . . It's just my girlfriend's out in the car, and we're getting a bit desperate . . .
BOOKSELLER: Hmm. Have you tried the service station just out there?
MAN: Oh. No. But are you sure you couldn't just lend me one?
BOOKSELLER: Sorry, no . . . Try the service station.
MAN: OK. Thanks . . . Better run.

Andrea Jutson: *Whitcoulls Bookshop, Auckland, New Zealand.*

EMAIL FROM CUSTOMER: Please, I would like to know if this book has any mildew smell. If not I will order it as soon as possible. I have one copy but don't like the smell. Thank you.

♦

CUSTOMER: This is John. John is five years old. He's hungry. Do you want to keep him?
BOOKSELLER: … ?!

Nina Grahmann: *Thalia Bookshop, Europa Passage, Hamburg, Germany.*

CUSTOMER: I've searched your Shakespeare section high and low, and I can't find a copy of *Of Mice and Men* anywhere.
BOOKSELLER: . . .

Tom Atherton: *Borders, Llantrisant, UK*

♦

BOY: Mummy, can I have this book?
WOMAN: Go and see if your dad will buy it for you.
BOY: Dad! Mummy says if you don't buy me this book, then you can't sleep in her bed tonight!

Eleanor Potten: *Book End, Bakewell, Derbyshire, UK*

CUSTOMER: Have you got *Merry Christmas, Mr Lawrence*?
BOOKSELLER *(pulling the book off the shelf)*: Sure. That will be £5.99, please.
WOMAN: . . . Hasn't he written anything cheaper?

Zoe King: *Hatchards, Ipswich, UK*

CUSTOMER: Do you have any *bookish* books?

Emma Milne-White: *The Hungerford Bookshop, Berkshire, UK*

CUSTOMER: I'd like to return this CD. It's scratched.
BOOKSELLER: It . . . you must have bought it next door.
(Customer looks around, surprised.)
CUSTOMER: Oh, this isn't HMV! Where's HMV gone?
BOOKSELLER: . . . It's still next door.

♦

CUSTOMER: If I were to, say... meet the love of my life in this bookshop, what section do you think they would be standing in?

Maria Duff: *Waterstone's, Scotch Hall, Drogheda, Ireland.*

CUSTOMER: Excuse me, I don't know the title, the author or what the book's about, but I know there were two words in the title . . .
BOOKSELLER: Ok, where did you see it?
CUSTOMER: Can't remember - please don't rush me. The two words were 'something' and 'something'.
BOOKSELLER: 'Something and something'? That doesn't ring a bell I'm afraid, do you remember what the book looked like?
CUSTOMER: Can't you just search for it?
BOOKSELLER: But . . . I don't have anything to search for.
CUSTOMER: *(Takes a pen and paper)* Look, just type this '. . . . . And . . . . .' into the computer. I can't believe you are so stupid!

Former bookseller: *Waterstone's, UK*

CUSTOMER: Do you know of any shop near here which might sell bibles?
BOOKSELLER: . . . yes.
CUSTOMER: Where?
BOOKSELLER: Er . . . here.

David Rees: *Books Alive [Christian Bookshop], Brighton and Hove, UK*

♦

CUSTOMER *(upon entering)*: So. What does this shop do?
BOOKSELLER: We're a bookshop. We sell books.
CUSTOMER: Oh. How does that work?
BOOKSELLER: Err . . .

Tanya Caunce, *TLC Books, Manly, Queensland, Australia.*

CUSTOMER *(pointing at the cover of Perdido Street Station by China Miéville)*: Excuse me, how do you pronounce this writer's name?
BOOKSELLER: Well, I've heard people say Mee-ville, but I think, because of the accent, it's Me-eh-ville.
CUSTOMER: No, I mean his first name.
BOOKSELLER: . . . Well, it's, *China* – like the country.
CUSTOMER: The country?
BOOKSELLER: . . .

Sophie Mayer: *Clerkenwell Tales, London, UK.*

CUSTOMER *(an elderly lady with Dutch accent)*: Do you have any books around here?
BOOKSELLER: Um, yes.
CUSTOMER: Where?
BOOKSELLER: Um, well, everywhere…
CUSTOMER: I don't understand. Where is books?
ANOTHER BOOKSELLER: Ah. I think she is looking for Boots – you know, the *chemist* . . .
BOOKSELLER: Oh!

Martin Brailli: *Waterstone's, Reading, UK*

CUSTOMER (*holding a copy of 'Inside WikiLeaks')*: What about this *Willileaks* book, is it any good?
BOOKSELLER: Um, do you mean *Wikileaks*? *Willileaks* is a topic I have little to no knowledge about.

Jamaica Zuanetti: *Berkelouw Books, Melbourne, Australia.*

CUSTOMER: I don't know why she wants it, but my wife asked for a copy of *The Dinosaur Cookbook.*
BOOKSELLER: *The Dinah Shore Cookbook*?
CUSTOMER: That must be it; I wondered what she was up to.

Elizabeth Durand: *Bookland of Maine, USA.*

CUSTOMER: The things on the walls...
BOOKSELLER: Bookshelves?
CUSTOMER: Yes.
(Pause.)
CUSTOMER: Do people still have them in their homes?
BOOKSELLER: Yes, I think so.
CUSTOMER: My friend's just made some - would you be able to sell them for him?

♦

(An old lady approaches the till)
CUSTOMER: Yes? What do you want?
BOOKSELLER: Erm, I rather thought that I might be able to help you.
CUSTOMER: Don't be ridiculous. Do I look as if I need ***your*** help . . .?

♦

CUSTOMER: I've just discovered that I'm Brad Pitt's sister and David Cameron's cousin. Is there a biography about me?

CUSTOMER: Would you mind if I had a little sleep on your sofa?

Hereward Corbett: *The Yellow-Lighted Bookshop, Gloucestershire, UK.*

CUSTOMER: Are there any cookbooks for people who don't like to cook, and who don't want to use many ingredients?
BOOKSELLER: I'm sure there are, let's have a search on the computer. I'll search 'simple food.'
CUSTOMER: I don't want any foreign food.
BOOKSELLER: Erm, OK, I'll try 'simple British food.'
CUSTOMER: Well, I've had those types of books before and they use things like olive oil. I don't want anything with olive oil in it.
BOOKSELLER: Erm . . .
CUSTOMER: Can you just type in 'cooking with lard,' and see what comes up?

Sara Waddington: *Simply Books, Pocklington, Yorkshire, UK.*

MAN: Hi, do you have my wife in here?
BOOKSELLER: Erm, I have lots of wives in here, what does yours look like?
MAN: She's let herself go a bit, is short and her roots are showing
BOOKSELLER: . . . !

Elizabeth Hurley: *Hurley Books, Mevagissy, Cornwall, UK*

CUSTOMER: Does this book come in other versions?
BOOKSELLER: I can check on the computer for you.
CUSTOMER: It's just that I don't like the way that this one pans out.

CUSTOMER: Do you have this book in stock? *(Shows Amazon print out)*
BOOKSELLER: We don't, I'm sorry. It looks to me that it was only published in America . . .
CUSTOMER: But I checked online and it said you had it.
BOOKSELLER: Ah, on our website?
CUSTOMER: You have a website?

Nia Rosser: *Waterstone's, Cardiff, UK.*

CUSTOMER: How much is this book?
BOOKSELLER: $6.
CUSTOMER: I don't want to pay that much. Will you take $2?
BOOKSELLER: No, the price is not negotiable.
CUSTOMER: I've got some cabbage in the truck, would you take some of that instead?
BOOKSELLER: . . . No.
CUSTOMER: How about some potatoes?
BOOKSELLER: No . . . what? . . . How is that different?

Caitlin Fry: *Jeff's Books, Strathalbyn, Australia.*

N.B. Pets with Tourette's is a thoroughly silly book with photos of cute animals with speech bubbles featuring horribly naughty phrases

CUSTOMER *(inspecting the book)*: Oh. That isn't what I was expecting.
BOOKSELLER: Yeah, it is a bit different to what we usually have in stock but. . .
CUSTOMER: No, I meant that I thought the book was about real people's pets, who have actual Tourette's.
BOOKSELLER: Like talking animals?
CUSTOMER *(seriously)*: Yes. That would have been better.

Sarah Chapman: *Well Read Bookshop, Newcastle, UK.*

CUSTOMER: I need to buy a present for my grandson. Apparently I need book number four.
BOOKSELLER: Book number four? Of which series?
CUSTOMER: Number four. That's all I know. Can you just show me where that would be?
BOOKSELLER: Well, there are lots of children's series with four books or more . . .
CUSTOMER: Can you just show me where I might find it?
(The bookseller takes the customer to the children's section)
BOOKSELLER: As you can see, there are lots of series . . .
CUSTOMER: Yes, but the book I want has number four written on it. Look, this one has number four. (*Points to fourth book of 'Series of Unfortunate Events'*)
BOOKSELLER: . . .
CUSTOMER: I'll take this one.
BOOKSELLER: Okay, but . . . never mind.

Georgi Paech: *Dillons Norwood Bookshop, Adelaide, Australia.*

♦

CUSTOMER: Do you sell bath plugs?

Simon Curtis: *Quagga Rare Books, Stellenbosch, South Africa.*

CUSTOMER: I've got an aubergine and I don't know what to do with it.
BOOKSELLER: Oh, well, what did you buy that for?
CUSTOMER: I didn't – someone gave it to me and I just saw you've got cups and saucers in the window – do you know about cooking?
BOOKSELLER: . . . Our window display is the Mad Hatter's tea party from Alice in Wonderland.

Katie Clapham: *Storytellers, Inc., St. Annes-on-Sea, Lancashire, UK.*

♦

CUSTOMER: Can I borrow your stapler?
BOOKSELLER: Sure. (*Puts the stapler on the counter and returns to pricing books*)
Customer immediately walks out of the shop with the stapler.
Bookseller walks to the door to see if customer is stapling something just outside.
Customer is walking off down the street.
BOOKSELLER *(chases after the customer):* Umm, can I have my stapler back?
CUSTOMER: Oh, I thought it was mine. The stapler I'd lost.
BOOKSELLER: Hmm . . . *(grabs stapler and returns to shop)*

Katherine FitzHywel: *The Grumpy Swimmer Bookshop, Melbourne, Australia.*

CUSTOMER: Oh, look, these books are all signed. *(Pause)* I wonder who signed them?

♦

CUSTOMER *(pointing back and forth from the bookseller to a full-size cut out of Legolas)*: Is that you?
BOOKSELLER: No. That's Orlando Bloom.

♦

PARENT *(to a child who is misbehaving)*: THERE SHOULD BE NO YELLING UNLESS SOMEONE IS ON FIRE!
CHILD *(firing back immediately)*: What if a weasel was robbing the store?
PARENT *(long pause, . . with the flickering of a smile)*: I don't know . . . is he armed?

Richard Due & Elizabeth Prouty: *Second Looks Books, Prince Frederick, Maryland, USA*

CUSTOMER *(offering plain brown paper bag to the bookseller with a friendly look in his eyes)*: Would you like a magic mushroom?
BOOKSELLER: . . .

Chris Howard: *Hay Cinema Bookshop, Hay-On-Wye, Powys, UK.*

(phone rings)
BOOKSELLER: Hello, Waterstone's, how can I help?
CUSTOMER: Hello? Yes I'm trying to cook this chicken.
BOOKSELLER: OK . . . what seems to be the issue?
CUSTOMER: Well, it says to cook it for two hours but I don't know if that's for if it's fresh or for if it's frozen.
BOOKSELLER: Interesting. Well I'm not sure I'm best qualified to answer that query.
CUSTOMER: Is there someone there who can?'

Will Goldstone: *Waterstone's, Bournemouth, UK*

♦

CUSTOMER: Is this a call centre?

Bruno Batista: *Chapters Bookstore, Dublin, Ireland.*

CUSTOMER: I want to buy a book for my mother. She likes Danielle Steel.
BOOKSELLER: Here she is, under 'S' for Steel.
CUSTOMER: . . . Well, I don't know which ones she's already read . . . Do you?
BOOKSELLER: . . .

Eve Taggart: *Half-Price Books, Atlanta, Georgia, USA.*

CUSTOMER *(holding up the carrier bag the bookseller has just given him)*: Can I use this for watering my plants?

Lena Goermann: *Thalia Bookshop, Hamburg, Germany.*

♦

CUSTOMER: Do you have this children's book I've heard about? It's supposed to be very good. It's called 'Lionel Richie and the Wardrobe.'

Sean Martin: *Primrose Hill Books, London, UK.*

CUSTOMER: Do you sell ice cubes?
BOOKSELLER: No.
CUSTOMER: Could I not even have three?
BOOKSELLER: No.
CUSTOMER: Two then? Just to chill some wine…
BOOKSELLER: We don't sell ice cubes.
CUSTOMER: What, none at all?
BOOKSELLER: No.
CUSTOMER: Oh.
BOOKSELLER *(sarcastically)*: Why not try the bookshop up the road, though?
CUSTOMER: Oh, OK then, I'll do that.
BOOKSELLER: . . . ?

CUSTOMER *(having read the blurb to Percy Jackson and the Lightning Thief aloud to his son)*: Excuse me, is this book based on a true story?
BOOKSELLER: It's about an American teenager discovering he's the son of Poseidon by accidentally vaporising his maths teacher.
CUSTOMER: Yes.
BOOKSELLER: So, no.

♦

CUSTOMER: Excuse me, I think you need to do something about your floor.
BOOKSELLER: Oh really? What seems to be the problem?
CUSTOMER: It's too high.
BOOKSELLER: I'm very sorry, no one's ever complained about that before.
(Five minutes later)
CUSTOMER: Me again. On closer inspection, I think the floor is fine.
BOOKSELLER: Great. Thanks for letting me know.
CUSTOMER: But your shelves are too low.

CUSTOMER: Can you point me to your military history section, please?
BOOKSELLER: I'm afraid we're such a small shop that we don't actually have one.
CUSTOMER: WHAT? No war section AT ALL? Have you no respect for the fallen?
BOOKSELLER: I can order in any title you're after. Or you'll find a decent selection of war poetry and novels inspired by war.
CUSTOMER *(ignoring this)*: You mean to tell me you have no shelf on weaponry?
BOOKSELLER: I'm afraid not.
CUSTOMER: Are you a pacifist or something?

♦

CUSTOMER: Can I have a copy of *Black Beauty*, please?
BOOKSELLER: Of course. You'll find a variety of different editions in the children's section.
CUSTOMER *(returning with three in her hand)*: I'll have this one *(hands over a hardback version)*. I wonder who wrote the other two . . .

Sarah Henshaw: *The Book Barge, Barton Marina, Staffordshire, UK.*

ACKNOWLEDGEMENTS:

Oodles of thanks to my wonderful agent, Charlie Campbell, who used to be a bookseller in Paris. He once served a customer who spat cheese soufflé all over him. He still doesn't know why they did that.

Many thanks to my lovely editor, Hugh Barker, who used to work at Ripping Yarns.

Big love to Greg for the wonderful illustrations, especially for the crucified bunny rabbit.

Many thanks to Jamie and Morag and the rest of the lovely people of Constable and Robinson and Ed Victor Ltd.

Thanks and love to Vanessa, Malcolm, Becky, Polly [and Magnus], and to Celia, Sasha, Sherry, Marie, Gloria, Lucinda and Zoe.

Thank you to the booksellers who submitted their own 'Weird Things.' It was heart-warming [and hilarious] to confirm that customers are saying strange things in bookshops worldwide.

Many thanks to Neil Gaiman and all the wonderful people of Twitter who enjoyed, and spread the word about, 'Weird Things.'

Thanks to everyone at H.tv. [Thank you Jo and Lotty.]

Thanks and love to my wonderful friends and family. [Thank you Dan and Nick.]

Thank you Miles. x

BOOKSELLER: Can I help you at all?
CUSTOMER: No, I don't think you're qualified. I need a psychiatrist; that's the only help I need.
BOOKSELLER: . . . OK.

Rachele Willey: *Waterstone's, East Grinstead, UK*

Simm

0737 61396
70

Sue's mobile
07768 040 645